Susan Maurer seals the broken heart in a snowdance that startles as it falls. Her poems cascade in suspense, like shadows in a blizzard. —STAR BLACK

Glossary of terms found in this catalog

Photography

Oil paint

Illegal act: Self-portrait backing a Pollock
© 2006

Raptor
Rhapsody, Deep, Blue
Rapture

Poems by Susan Maurer

POETS WEAR PRADA • Hoboken, New Jersey

Raptor Rhapsody

Copyright © 2007 Susan Maurer

Poets Wear Prada
533 Bloomfield Street, Second Floor
Hoboken, New Jersey 07030

http://pwpbooks.blogspot.com

First North American Publication 2007
First Mass Market Paperback Edition 2013

Grateful acknowledgment to *Confrontation*, *Fire*, *Hawaii Review*, *Haz Mat*, *Moon*, *Skidrow Penthouse*, *Spiky Palm* and Poetz.com where some of these poems previously appeared.

ISBN-13: 978-0615650197
ISBN-10: 0615650198

Printed in the U.S.A.

Front Cover Design: Roxanne Hoffman & Susan Maurer
Fly Leaf Collage: *Illegal act: Self-portrait licking a Pollack* by Erik La Prade
Back Cover Author Photo: Patricia Carragon

For Florynce Kennedy

Table of Contents

I am passionately opposed to the notion held for so long that women's true subjects are "love and loss."
　　　　　　—CAROLYN KIZER, *100 Great Poems by Women*

Perhaps you disagree with the results...
I encourage you to keep on reading, however.
　　　　　　—PATRICK J. CARNES, *The Betrayal Bonds*

Half King

The crush kicked in
at Half King. Just the way
you were sitting, right shoulder
forward, expectant, as if I
just might say the best thing
and it has all turned to paper,
cyberspace, a collection of
letters shaped into words, letters
kneaded like dough to turn into
little houses of words.

Bird

My talent has returned, biding bird.
Back from deserting sojourn
leaving me calling "Bird here bird,
won't you come back?"

Rice

I memorized the way you ate rice.
It was nice.
If tested on how you handle CDs
I'm A+.
I've taped every minute, word and now hope
you don't change up to grab rice from my eyes and say
GIMME BACK THE RICE YOUR EYES STOLE
YOU BITCH.

Wild Horses

I'm falling in love.
Don't tell anyone.
Not even the wild horses
which will be sent.
These feelings, such
a torrent.
Who can stop them?
At flood I am
at least no longer
outside looking in.
I needed you so bad
before I knew your name.
O if you've a manicured life
you'll
turn away as I half wish
I could.

When fruition comes
the umbilicus stem
snaps the fruit to ground.
to rot to open up to seeds
to green, to grow.

Blossom

Want my wanting
on ice? Always frozen
something to admire, the
shapes it takes. Well, what's
in it for me? Keeps you around
and me hoping for that melt
into a martini, that gin bite.
I
think about the time in Ireland
we took the kids' baseballs
and had a martini party,
ended up playing midnight
baseball on the tennis court
lit by rings of headlights.

Blue Rose

Drop. Drop.

From the eyedropper
　　　to the top of the glass
　of water
　　　　　as the doctor says
　and the blue
　　　　liquid spreads out
　　　and blossoms like a rose...

Eric/k

You're getting ready to leave
and you put on the black leather jacket
and you sling on that literary bag
that guys like you carry,
across one shoulder, across the chest,
resting on the opposite hip
and I sort of, well actually
back you up in a corner and yell
"Aren't you gonna give me a hug?'
and you do and actually add
a sweet little kiss right on my lips.

Breathe

Every blade of grass has its Angel that bends over it and whispers,
"Grow, grow." —Talmud

Stark, staring angels, two, wring
their hands at what unreels,
unspools, spins from the wheel,
from the spider's spinneret,
opens, sluices, sluices, sluices the
way life sluices, the way
rain fills the rain spout
and sluices torrential to the
dirt below. They witness
the grasses' growth, they
feel the agony when evil
cries, they feel the pain of the mad dog slain,
the run that Grendel,
one arm hewn, makes,
gushing, to the fen. They
witness, and feel the pain
of evil's death every bit
as simple as death of a rabbit on
the road. It is too late to escape.
All left is witness, empathy,
unfleeing from the instances of pain of death
the last attempt to breath.

Stradivarius

You are our instrument.
I dial the number
hand you the telephone.
You tell me he says
"I got your letter,"
You chuckle, repeat.
He "And I forgive you."
And he asks
"Is Anthony there?"
And I say
"I did him twice last night"
and you convulse with laughter,
say "No you didn't."
And he says
"There'll be reprisals."
And I want you to
tell him the turkey was good
but you two begin talking of other things.

You're playing our song.

Subject:

I take the phone off the hook
to stop the sound of silence.
It can't come in unless you invite it.
Funny how the index finger
can turn into a sword you throw yourself on,
no one home.

Gamelan

Erased him from my address book,
    the stages were worryworryworry
    and surmise
Ended by machine, abrupt,
    ran for my psychological life.
The stages were ratiocinationratiocination
    and fear, actually.
Could I—would I—try again?

And damn the person who said
    "Go ahead, whatever happens you
    write so well about love."

Salad Flowers

for Eva Slamova, Thanksgiving '02

So we are joined by the sin
of orchidicide,
fleur murderers…
I slice the fuschia shape in
half. We ate.
Cannibals we are.

It makes our petals shiver.

Broadway Boheme Update:
5-23-03: Pink Beret

I've been somewhat shaky in my words
this past few days
so I am glad to go with Tom
to see the dancing fog, snow
which flutters mothlike to the stage,
fire—a black clad man
crouched behind the stove, waving flashlights,
orange-beamed, round and round.
O this modern day Boheme,
the saga of the pink beret
(on sale for thirty plus as souvenir),
red velvet clothes, bloodless death by cough.
I wash my eyes with tears
at love's last breath. Lucky her who does not
live to grieve.

Snowdance: Entropalizomeno

It is not good to be alone when it snows slow long strong. Silence can kill so talk on the phone or visit neighbors. —Hazel Tree

Over the intimate pain of a stomach ache
I realize there is something to be done
other than keep on, anyway.
Simple Tums. (I buy Tums.)
The clowns are planted
and I think how sometimes
Eva just doesn't understand.
Like how snowfall's like orgasm,
contained, dancing.
We argue about that.
Well oh, hers is the most recent
experience, that, with the thrum of a man
whereas I am back to mechanical devices
having thrown him out or
let him go like that fucking seagull
they say that if you love it let it go.

Flasher: Passer

My dreamy parkcoffee mornings
have become less pleasant since
I've been hassled by a flasher.
Caught me twice.

I've called the cops and told park authorities.
It's not that I fear death by dick sight
but it is distinctly not cool.
The third time he sat near
I just continued to feed Passer
(a little sparrow) and he turned up his
boombox to get me to look and so on.

Next time he stormed by with an angry look on his face
I suppose because I didn't look.

Passer is so cute, jumps up,
takes tiny bits of bread from my hand
and today she revealed what makes her so cheeky.
She has a baby to feed so cute; that was a better morning.

Told Eric who got quite steamy
wanted details. (The dick was huge,
limp and seemed to be coated with baby oil.)
Eric told me his flashing was not going well,
maybe he needed some baby oil.
I mailed him some baby oil and
he was quite incensed I would do
something so unmaidenly.

I haven't laughed so hard in ages.
I needed a good laugh.

Also by Susan Maurer

Perfect Dark
Lund, Sweden: Ungoverable Press, 2009

Raw Poems
Randolph, MA: Gold Wake Press, 2008

Maerchen
New York: Maverick Duck Press, 2008

in2
with Mark Sonnenfeld
East Windsor, NJ: Marymark Press, 2005

The Longing
New York: Center for Book Arts, 2005

Dream Addict
Ellsworth, ME: Backwood Broadsides, 2004

Heat Ghosts
with Tom Savage, and Merry Fortune
New York: Quarter Horse Press, 2003

Three Poems by Susan Maurer
Santa Rosa, CA: Clamshell Press, 2002

Pawdy-do Sank-ee oon-Twah
with Bill Kushner, and Tom Savage
New York: Quarter Horse Press, 1998

By the Blue Light of the Morning Glory
New York: Linear Arts, 1997

About the Author

Susan Maurer's full-length collection, *Perfect Dark,* was published by Ungovernable Press (Lund, Sweden: 2009). Her two most recent chapbooks are *Raw Poems* from Gold Wake Press (Randolph, MA: 2008) and *Maerchen* from Maverick Duck Press (New York: 2008). Other chapbooks have been published by Linear Arts, Marymark Press and Backwood Broadsides. Letterpress broadsides were done by Clamshell Press and The Center for Book Arts. Her poetry has been nominated five times for Pushcart, published in 15 countries, and has appeared in over 400 magazines and anthologies, including *Off the Cuffs: Poetry by and about the Police* (New York: Softskull Press, 2003), *Help Yourself!* (New York: Autonomedia, 2001), *Virginia Quarterly Review, Literary Imagination, Cross Connect, Isle, Orbis,* and *Volt.* Her full-length book, several of her chaps and broadsides, as well as recordings of her readings and interviews are archived at the Poetry Collection & Literary Archives at the University at Buffalo (SUNY) and at NYU Fales, among other places.

She participated in a *Rattapallax* CD, and posed and read for photographer Anna Siano's INSIDE-OUT Photography & Poetry Project showcased at Hoboken's 2006 Artists Studio Tour. Composer David Morneau set a poem by Maurer to music for *Love Songs,* an on-going song cycle project that pairs sonnets by William Shakespeare with poems by contemporary writers. Their collaboration was premiered in December of 2010 at The Tank in New York with a performance by Mary Hubbell (soprano), Roberta Michel (flute) and Ernesto Ramos (guitar). Maurer has read at Poets House, St. Mark's Poetry Project, Bowery Poetry Club, on the Brooklyn Bridge with the Unbearables, as well as at the National Arts Club, Harvard Coop, Barnes & Noble Booksellers, and the Susquehanna Art Museum, among other venues.

www.ingramcontent.com/pod-product-compliance
Lightning Source LLC
Chambersburg PA
CBHW041800040426
42447CB00001B/40

9 780615 650197

About the Author

Susan Maurer's full-length collection, *Perfect Dark*, was published by Ungovernable Press (Lund, Sweden: 2009). Her two most recent chapbooks are *Raw Poems* from Gold Wake Press (Randolph, MA: 2008) and *Maerchen* from Maverick Duck Press (New York: 2008). Other chapbooks have been published by Linear Arts, Marymark Press and Backwood Broadsides. Letterpress broadsides were done by Clamshell Press and The Center for Book Arts. Her poetry has been nominated five times for Pushcart, published in 15 countries, and has appeared in over 400 magazines and anthologies, including *Off the Cuffs: Poetry by and about the Police* (New York: Softskull Press, 2003), *Help Yourself!* (New York: Autonomedia, 2001), *Virginia Quarterly Review*, *Literary Imagination*, *Cross Connect*, *Isle*, *Orbis*, and *Volt*. Her full-length book, several of her chaps and broadsides, as well as recordings of her readings and interviews are archived at the Poetry Collection & Literary Archives at the University at Buffalo (SUNY) and at NYU Fales, among other places.

She participated in a *Rattapallax* CD, and posed and read for photographer Anna Siano's INSIDE-OUT Photography & Poetry Project showcased at Hoboken's 2006 Artists Studio Tour. Composer David Morneau set a poem by Maurer to music for *Love Songs,* an on-going song cycle project that pairs sonnets by William Shakespeare with poems by contemporary writers. Their collaboration was premiered in December of 2010 at The Tank in New York with a performance by Mary Hubbell (soprano), Roberta Michel (flute) and Ernesto Ramos (guitar). Maurer has read at Poets House, St. Mark's Poetry Project, Bowery Poetry Club, on the Brooklyn Bridge with the Unbearables, as well as at the National Arts Club, Harvard Coop, Barnes & Noble Booksellers, and the Susquehanna Art Museum, among other venues.

www.ingramcontent.com/pod-product-compliance
Lightning Source LLC
Chambersburg PA
CBHW041800040426
42447CB00001B/40